Wa(o)ndering To Poetry

Lyla Fain Osmundsen

To Gwen!
My friend
and fighting for our
planet together
Love,
Lyla

Text copyright © 2018 Lyla Fain Osmundsen
Cover illustration copyright © 2018 Lyla Fain Osmundsen
Photo by Lyle Eugene Osmundsen
All rights reserved
No part of this book may be reproduced, or stored in a retrieval system, or transmitted in any form or by any means, electronic, mechanical, photocopying, recording, or otherwise, without express written permission of the publisher.
Publisher: June Sound Swirls <lylafo1.gmail.com>
ISBN-13: 978-1717396556
ISBN-10: 1717396550

Dedication

To my parents, Alice Fain and Lyle Eugene (Bud), who told me fascinating bedtime stories and read my favorite books to me, inviting me to open my mind and heart to the world. The best gift our parents gave to me, my two brothers, and sister was time. They listened and answered our questions. I love and miss them for all the other gifts which they gave to each other and their four children.

Lyla Fain Osmundsen

Acknowledgements

Thank you Monday night writers group: Dianne, Anne, Danae, Lynnea, Laurayne, Valarie, Marilyn, Donna, and Joyce for creative, technical and laughter support. With Danae's "Self-Publishing Series" and Dianne's and Anne's thoughtful editing, along with their patience, encouragement, and chocolate, my book is published. Love and gratitude to Chuck, for his smiles, shoulder massages, and love.

Lyla Fain Osmundsen

Family

Alice

A tiny girl in a white dress
sits on her back-porch steps,
listening to her Mama's friend, Mag,
tell her stories;
breathing in patience, humility, wonder.

Twelve-year-old Alice cringes,
as her mother gives household belongings
to visitors who admire various items.

Gracious, generous Hermione, eyes smiling,
presents her daughter a nourishing childhood
of surprises, and mouthwatering southern meals;
gifting rich family tapestry.

Daddy John, pipe-fitter by trade, travels through
the south,
winding sweet home to wife and child.
Wages turn into dresses, books, The Woman's
College of Georgia tuition.
Quietly thoughtful, he believes,
"Alice is perfect in every way."

Lyle

Lyle, handsome, smart, almost loses his way
to become Alice's husband.
Two streets, same name, two hours late for their
first date.
Army Air Corps soldier successfully navigates to
marriage
and a law degree.

Wonderland

Slipped down a portal
and bounced out into your warm hug,
lingered on the plains,
learning patience, to an extent,
climbed hills, then mountains,
following your maps and directions;
dodged some faults, descended deep valleys,
your wisdom in my pocket.

Two and Two

Alice becomes mother at twenty upon Lyla's
appearance.
John invades just one and a half years later.
Karen floats down with sweet nature after six
years.
David, wisdom wrapped in wrinkled, baby body,
completes family and his oldest sister learns
the delights and challenges of child care.

Mama and Daddy in love survive
four children who hug, fight, and
care for each other;
becoming a teacher, business manager, nurse
practitioner, and accountant.

Lyla Fain Osmundsen

Me

Phasing

Moonrise, consistent glow
of childhood,
assures me
I am.

Moon waxing,
presents perplexing puzzle.
Who am I?
Wearing parent charm, friend ornament;
admiring, coveting,
losing, gifting,
refusing, accepting,
borrowing, creating,
in turn.

Moon waning
reflects a question;
illuminating the answer
known as a child.

Who Is Going to Stop Me?

I see critics over there.
I hear critics everywhere.
The strongest critic
is right in my chair!

People opinion politely or not.
The Who, who stops me, isn't another,
but myself who smothers!

Most critics comment on one or two
unfavorable traits.
My inner critic examines
every move I make!

Teacher

Yesterday a teacher came
again to lay the track.
Finger strain, aching back
shape a flexible musical rack.

Met the notes E, G, finally F;
the terms bar, staff, measure, treble clef.
Master three notes, two chords;
focus fifteen minutes times two, maybe more.

Practice, play.
Music worth the fine,
when I strum a guitar tune for the first time!

End Play

She performed to please her audience,
to receive their favorable reviews.
When there was no applause,
she frowned or teared in fear
of losing her expected fans.
For many years, star of the same drama,
reviving the old script again and again,
until she stepped off the stage
and wrote to please herself.

Lyla Fain Osmundsen

Love

Lyla Fain Osmundsen

Here Now Perfect We

Colorful, precise art;
stroked by clarity;
awash in empathy;
metaphorically painting
the landscape of our lives.

Waiting

The red-tailed hawk sits patiently in her tree,
watching, waiting,
just like me,
but we differ in our drive.
Survival is her goal,
acceptance, mine.
She observes for hours.
I sit, hold my breath a bit,
then dive to the laptop or phone.
She flies to another high perch.
I drift inside my head.
Her eyes alert for prey,
mine wary of loss;
both uncertain at this moment.

Stained Glass Marriage Celebration

Swirls of color, textured, sparkling;
bound in structure, yet fluid.
Tuned to love, to life.
Undulating toward bursts of
red, gold, icy crystal;
soft, rosy mauve ribbons
through cobalt sea.

From glass shards, precisely edged,
a symphony of celebration;
song of trust and hope;
joy of duo realized
in solo artist vision.

Mountain Sides

Only two hours and ninety-six miles;
flew over those tips; easily caressed those curves,
for awhile.
Heedless of speed, ignoring sign;
rushed to the poet's corner for more rhyme.
What trail now through maze of rock and soft snow?
Where is the path beyond the wind moan?
Which side of the mountain is home?

Wa(o)nder

Senses on high alert;
colors blinding;
wonder, wander;
soft blanket safe.
Oh!
Wake up shattered.
Night dreams scattered.

Meet Me At The Golden Mean

He said.
She said.
They said simultaneously,
meet me in the middle.
Searching for the peace place;
looking for the happy spot;
yearning for the win-win;
recalculate, rethink, regroup;
no turning away;
no running from;
this time finding gold
means staying.

Lyla Fain Osmundsen

Friends

Margaret Dance

Without a melody your lyrics invite a dance.
You illustrate form with colorful vision
to beginners in a tiny classroom.
Your rhythm refuses to settle,
traveling gracefully through
laughter and silliness,
sadness and tears;
performing passion for life;
dancing, drawing, being,
peace.

Nellie

Giggling with her eyes,
enticing me back in time with her tales;
white cloud curls framing her mischievous face,
my friend, Nellie, gives me comfort and laughter.
Although her coffee is weak,
her opinions are strong,
as is her life-long passion for sweets.
Devoted to family,
delighted by garden bloom;
secure in her birth city;
she transforms crossing our street
into an adventure.

Summer Friendship

Another summer burns into autumn.
You pack once again for the warm winter home,
 yet adventure sharing continues.
We visit virtually via text and voice;
continuing our thread of listening, laughing,
comforting, understanding;
forthright in valuing our age and experience
as women.

Moments

Heart Sick

Light, translucent truth,
swiftly falling to shadow.
Confusion, fear reign.

Ahora/Now

Sombra a luz,/Shadow to light,
gris a oro,/gray to gold,
pensando a siendo./thinking to being.

March

Golden-grey cloud sky,
flowing over foothills, spreads
gold leaf to tree tops.

Beams

Heat blanket smothers
budding earth surface.
Eye of sky radiates
upon sweating planet
and beams.

Spring Morning

Watched a yellow-black butterfly
flutter to the blackberry bushes.
Witnessed a frenetic hummingbird
race between two closely spaced tree branches,
dropping abruptly to rest on a red camellia.
Heard insistent duck quacks from the creek.
Spotted ninety-four-year-old, Nellie,
my friend and neighbor,
wandering about the patio next to my house.
Answering my, "Whatcha doin?",
she displayed a small bouquet of
Cecil Bruner roses from my rose tree.
"Easier to reach from this side", she grinned.

Silent, Still

Silent, star-filled night,
brightens to peaceful dawn.
Bird song gone;
no scent of fragrant blossom.

Yelling Is Unproductive

Yelling is unproductive.
Knowing this very well;
why still engage in outrage;
loud speech deafening the enough bell?

ACCOMPLISHED LIST.
Much more gratifying than a to-do list, don't you think?

Thanks for your poems! My favorites

p. 19 & p. 32
the Golden Mean — Yelling

Linda

courtyard.com

Amuse

Capricious player,
littering laughter,
mixing it up.
Witty, wise jester,
protecting fun.
Joker, wag, clown,
conjuring smiles, banishing frowns.
Antics, based upon amuse,
turn hate to humor,
humanity to infuse.
Always a play, a poem, a dance or musical art,
creating one way to a kind understanding in a fear-filled heart.

Lyla Fain Osmundsen

About the Author

Born and raised in the foothills of Georgia, Lyla Fain Osmundsen began writing diaries, journals, and poems around the age of twelve. She accepted a full scholarship to The Woman's College of Georgia by agreeing to teach in Georgia's public schools for five years after receiving her degree. Love and life intervened during those years and, before moving to California, she acquired a Special Education credential and a husband. Prior to retiring, she taught reading, math, and language skills in California public schools and at a California Youth Authority Fire Camp. In retirement she lives in the California foothills, inspired by the creek in her backyard; literary, performance, and fine arts; and protection of human rights and the fragile eco system of this wondrous planet.

Made in the USA
Middletown, DE
10 August 2018